Annie Deluxe Souvenir Edition

Original Broadway production photos by Martha Swope

Television production photos © ABC Photography Archives

ISBN 0-634-05835-5

HAL•LEONARD®
CORPORATION

7777 W. BLUEMOUND RD. P.O. BOX 13819 MILWAUKEE, WI 53213

In Australia Contact:
Hal Leonard Pty. Ltd.
22 Taunton Drive P.O. Box 5130
Cheltenham East, 3192 Victoria, Australia
Email: ausadmin@halleonard.com

For all works contained herein:
Unauthorized copying, arranging, adapting, recording or public performance is an infringement of copyright.
Infringers are liable under the law.

Visit Hal Leonard Online at
www.halleonard.com

Annie Original Broadway Production

Annie

Annie Original Broadway Production

Annie

Annie The Motion Picture

Annie

Annie The Motion Picture

Annie

Annie The Television Production

Annie

Annie The Television Production

ACT ONE

It is December of 1933 and America is deep in the midst of the Great Depression. On the Lower East Side of New York, the Municipal Orphanage, Girls' Annex, has been the drab home of eleven-year-old Annie for all but the first two months of her life, when she was left on the front steps of the Orphanage with an unsigned note saying, "Please take care of our little darling. Her name is Annie … We have left half of a silver locket around her neck and kept the other half so that when we come back for her you will know that she's our baby." Early one chilly morning, awake at 4 am, Annie wonders what her lost parents might be like (MAYBE).

Miss Agatha Hannigan, the mean-tempered spinster who is in charge of the Orphanage, is furious at finding Annie and the Orphans awake at 4 am and puts them to work scrubbing the floor. Annie and the Orphans angrily lament the fact that they are living [IT'S] THE HARD-KNOCK LIFE. Later that morning, Annie seizes the opportunity to escape from the Orphanage by hiding in a laundry bag that is toted off into a truck. If her parents aren't coming back for her, Annie is going to find them.

In New York's St. Mark's Place, city dogcatchers pursue stray dogs, but they miss one, a sad-faced mutt that is immediately adopted by Annie, who has been wandering alone through the wintry streets of the city. "They're after me, too," Annie tells the dog, and then assures him that "Everything's gonna be fine for the both of us. If not today then… TOMORROW." Officer Ward of the NYPD suspects that Annie's dog is stray, but she tells him that the dog is hers: "I call him Sandy because of his nice sandy color." Sandy responds to his new name when he is called by Annie, and Officer Ward is reluctantly persuaded that the dog indeed belongs to Annie.

Underneath the 59th Street Bridge is a so-called Hooverville, a Depression-style shanty town that is home to an assortment of unemployed New Yorkers who sarcastically let it be known that WE'D LIKE TO THANK YOU HERBERT HOOVER. Annie turns up with Sandy, wondering if anyone in the Hooverville had ever left a baby at an orphanage. Her sunny disposition endears Annie to the Hooverville-ites, who invite her to join them in a cup of Mulligan stew. The police raid the Hooverville, and Annie is arrested, although Sandy escapes.

Back at the Orphanage, Miss Hannigan's nerves are at the breaking point from having to put up with LITTLE GIRLS when Officer Ward arrives with Annie in tow. After Officer Ward leaves, Miss Hannigan is about to clobber Annie when into the Orphanage comes Miss Grace Farrell, who is the young and beautiful private secretary to Oliver Warbucks, the billionaire industrialist. Warbucks has decided to invite an orphan to spend the Christmas holidays at home. And, to the fury of Miss Hannigan, Annie is chosen by Miss Farrell and driven off in a limousine.

Annie and Grace arrive at Warbucks's Fifth Avenue mansion, where a platoon of servants is busily cleaning. Annie is delighted to learn that, as a guest, she herself won't have to do any cleaning (I THINK I'M GONNA LIKE IT HERE).

Oliver Warbucks arrives home from a business trip and is unhappy to discover that the orphan invited by Grace isn't a boy. Still, he agrees to take Annie to the movies, to the Roxy Theatre, and Warbucks, Annie and Grace walk forty-five blocks to Times Square, through the streets of the city that Warbucks loves best (N.Y.C.). And, while walking with Annie, Warbucks finds himself unexpectedly growing to like her.

A week later, Grace Farrell turns up at the Orphanage to tell Miss Hannigan that Warbucks has decided to adopt Annie. Miss Hannigan is not happy about this news, to say the least. As Grace is leaving, she bumps into Miss Hannigan's ne'er-do-well con artist brother, Rooster, who is broke, just out of prison and looking for a handout from his sister. And with Rooster is his floozy girlfriend, Lily. Miss Hannigan, Rooster and Lily dream of better days for themselves on EASY STREET.

In his Fifth Avenue mansion, Warbucks is about to tell Annie that he wishes to adopt her. But he first gives her a present – a new locket from Tiffany's to replace the old, broken one she always wears. Annie, however, breaks down in tears – she doesn't want a new locket because the old locket had been left with her by her parents. And the one thing she wants in all the world is to find her mother and father. Crushed, stunned, Warbucks promises Annie that he'll find her parents for her. Grace and the Servants assure Annie that Warbucks will find her mother and father (YOU WON'T BE AN ORPHAN FOR LONG).

ACT TWO

In Rockefeller Center, on a radio program called "The Oxydent Hour of Smiles," starring Bert Healy, Warbucks offers a certified check of $50,000 to anyone who can prove that they are Annie's parents. Healy and the Boylan Sisters go off the air singing YOU'RE NEVER FULLY DRESSED WITHOUT A SMILE, a song that the Orphans hear over the radio in the Orphanage and imitate.

Later that night, Miss Hannigan has a pair of callers at the orphanage, Ralph and Shirley Mudge, a couple from Canada who claim to be Annie's parents. Miss Hannigan is astonished when the Mudges reveal themselves to be Rooster and Lily in disguise. Rooster offers to cut his sister in on the $50,000 reward money if she'll provide him and Lily with details they'll need to pass themselves off as Annie's parents. Miss Hannigan agrees to join the plot.

In Washington, at the White House, President Roosevelt and his Cabinet mirror the national gloom as they listen to a radio tirade against FDR. Warbucks arrives with Annie, who innocently blurts out to the glum group that things are bound to get better soon (Reprise: TOMORROW). Everyone, including the President, is turned optimistic by Annie's cheery spirits. A telegram arrives from New York saying that hundreds of couples claiming to be Annie's parents are jamming the streets outside Warbuck's mansion. Warbucks and Annie rush back to New York.

At the mansion, Grace sadly tells Warbucks and Annie that all of the couples who'd claimed to be her parents had turned out to be fakes— none of them knew about the locket. Alone with Annie, Warbucks tells her that before she came into his life SOMETHING WAS MISSING. Now, with seemingly no hope left of finding Annie's parents, Warbucks says to Annie that he'd like to adopt her. She's delighted, he's delighted, and they both joyfully agree that I DON'T NEED ANYTHING BUT YOU.

At a party in the mansion to celebrate the adoption, the happy Servants feel as though it's Christmas every day since Annie came along (ANNIE). As the adoption papers are about to be signed, Rooster and Lily, in their disguises as the Mudges, show up at the party and claim that Annie is their daughter. And they have a fake birth certificate to prove it, plus, thanks to Miss Hannigan's connivance, half of a silver locket that appears to fit Annie's half.

Warbucks is vaguely suspicious of them, however, and asks that they come back for Annie and the $50,000 the following morning, Christmas. The Mudges leave and Annie rushes upstairs in tears just as President Roosevelt pays a surprise call on Warbucks. Grace, half remembering that she'd bumped into Rooster at the Orphanage, tells Warbucks that there is something phony about the Mudges. Warbucks turns to Roosevelt for help from the FBI.

Christmas morning, 1933, in the Warbucks mansion. Warbucks, Grace and FDR have been up all night, in constant telephone contact with the FBI, and they have unhappy news for Annie – her mother and father died many years ago. But then who are Ralph and Shirley Mudge? And who knew about the locket? Miss Hannigan! The Orphans and Miss Hannigan arrive to spend Christmas at the mansion. Rooster and Lily, again in their disguises as the Mudges, come to collect Annie and the check for $50,000. But the jig is up – the Secret Service arrests Rooster, Lily and Miss Hannigan, who is dragged away screaming. A huge Christmas box arrives for Annie – in it is Sandy, who has been found for Warbucks by the police. Happy ending as Annie, Warbucks, Grace and all agree that this Christmas is the beginning of a wonderful new life for not only them but for everyone in America (A NEW DEAL FOR CHRISTMAS).

Charles Strouse

A long-standing member of the Songwriters Hall of Fame, and in January 2002, an inductee into The Theater Hall of Fame, Charles Strouse's first Broadway musical, *BYE BYE BIRDIE* (1960), won him a Tony Award and the London Critics Best Foreign Musical Award. In 1970, *APPLAUSE*, starring Lauren Bacall, achieved the same honors and his smash hit, *ANNIE* (1977), also won a Tony for Best Score as well as two Grammy Awards. Some of his other musicals include *ALL AMERICAN, GOLDEN BOY* (starring Sammy Davis Jr.), *IT'S A BIRD, IT'S A PLANE, IT'S SUPERMAN, I AND ALBERT,* directed in London by John Schlesinger, and *DANCE A LITTLE CLOSER*, written with Alan Jay Lerner. *CHARLIE & ALGERNON* won a 1981 Tony nomination for Best Score, as did *RAGS* in 1987 and *NICK AND NORA* in 1992. He wrote both the music and lyrics for off-Broadway's *MAYOR*, and teamed again with Martin Charnin to create *ANNIE WARBUCKS*, the sequel to *ANNIE*.

His film scores include *BONNIE & CLYDE, THE NIGHT THEY RAIDED MINSKY'S*, and *ALL DOGS GO TO HEAVEN*. *"Those Were The Days,"* the theme song for TV's *ALL IN THE FAMILY* is a Strouse song, with lyrics by his most frequent collaborator, Lee Adams. *"Born Too Late"*, a 1958 pop song written with Fred Tobias, was a top-10 BILLBOARD chart hit and is still heard on many oldies stations.

The quadruple platinum album title song by Jay-Z, *"Hard Knock Life (Ghetto Anthem)"*, won the 1999 Grammy for best Rap album, charted for more than a year and won the BILLBOARD 1998 R&B Album of the Year Award.

Strouse's far-ranging talents include chamber and orchestral works, a piano concerto, a two-piano sonata, and operas. His latest choral work, *"The Child in Us All"*, premiered in Spring 2000. *NIGHTINGALE,* an opera based on the Hans Christian Andersen story for which he wrote music, book and lyrics, was recorded by Sarah Brightman. Strouse was commissioned in 2001 to write *CONCERTO AMERICA* for the pianist Jeffrey Biegel. The work premiered in June of 2002 with the Boston Pops at Symphony Hall.

Charles Strouse created the ASCAP Musical Theatre Workshop in New York, where he encouraged the talents of countless young composers, writers and performers. In 1999, Strouse received the ASCAP Foundation Richard Rodgers Award for Career Lifetime Achievement in Musical Theatre.

In December 1995, a TV reinterpretation of the classic *BYE BYE BIRDIE* (starring Jason Alexander and pop-star Vanessa Williams) aired on ABC-TV. The 1995/96 Emmy for Outstanding Individual Achievement in Music and Lyrics was given to the new song written for and performed by Vanessa Williams: *"Let's Settle Down".* Another TV interpretation in 1999, *ANNIE,* aired on ABC's Wonderful World of Disney, swept the ratings by winning over 40 million viewers, won the 1999 Peabody Award for best TV musical, the 1999 TV Guide Award and 2 Emmy Awards. The show starred Kathy Bates, Audra McDonald, Alan Cumming, Kristin Chenoweth, Victor Garber, Andrea McArdle and Alicia Morton as Annie and ranked #1 as movie of the year.

A revised *GOLDEN BOY* was produced by the Long Wharf Theatre in New Haven (November 2000); and the *ENCORES! Series* presented the show in March 2002.

Future projects:

GOLDEN BOY will be performed at the Greenwich Theatre in England in June 2003.

THE NIGHT THEY RAIDED MINSKY'S, which Charles Strouse originally scored for film, has been turned into a full-length musical. The Broadway-bound version has a book by the late Michael Okrent and Evan Hunter, lyrics by Susan Birkenhead. The Manhattan Theatre Club has scheduled the show for its 2003-04 season.

An adaptation of the Paddy Chayevsky film *MARTY,* had a successful regional theatre run at the Huntington Theatre in Boston in September 2002. The show reunites Strouse with Lee Adams as lyricist; the book is by Rupert Holmes. John C. Reilly starred in the Huntington production and will again star when the show comes to Broadway next season.

Martin Charnin

The creator of **Annie**, Martin Charnin originated the role of "Big Deal" in the Broadway production of **West Side Story** in 1957. His Tony award-winning Broadway production of **Annie** (the 13th longest running American musical in Broadway history) celebrated its twentieth anniversary in 1997 with a return to Broadway, and this national company spent three years touring the United States. Another production closed in 2000 in the United Kingdom, having been nominated for the 1999 Olivier Award for Best Musical. A third production ended a two-year run in Amsterdam in 2000, and his 15th overall production recently closed after a triumphant 2-year run in Australia.

Mr. Charnin has been the director, lyricist, composer, librettist, producer or combination of the aforementioned for over 85 theatrical productions including **Annie**, **Annie - London** (1979), **London** (2000), **Australia** (2000), **Holland** (2000), **Annie Warbucks**, the rock opera version of **Joan of Arc**, **Mata Hara**, **Loose Lips**, **Star-Crossed**, **Sid Caesar & Company**, **Carnal Knowledge**, **In Persons** with Eli Wallach and Anne Jackson, **The Flowering Peach**, **Winchell**, the revised Goodspeed production of Cole Porter's **Can-Can** (for which he re-wrote the book), **Cafe Crown**, **Mike**, **Laughing Matters**, **The No-Frills Revue**, **Upstairs' at O'Neal's**, **The First**, **On the Swing Shift**, **A Little Family Business**, **The National Lampoon Show**, **Lena Horne: The Lady and Her Music**, **I Remember Mama**, **Hot Spot**, **Zenda**, **Put It in Writing**, **Fallout**, **Kaleidoscope**, **Ballad for a Firing Squad**, **La Strada**, **Nash at Nine**, **Two by Two** and also in London, **Bar Mitzvah Boy**, **Bless the Bride,** and **The 9 1/2 Quid Revue**.

His collaborations include Peter Allen, Harold Arlen, Vernon Duke, Keith Levensen, Marvin Hamlisch, Peter Sipos, Mary Rodgers, Richard Rodgers and Charles Strouse. He has directed Fred Astaire, Anne Bancroft, Lena Horne, Danny Kaye, Angela Landsbury, Johnny Mathis, Bill Murray, Bebe Neuwirth, Bernadette Peters, Sarah Jessica Parker, Gilda Radner, Molly Ringwald, Chita Rivera, Liv Ullman, Eli Wallach, Anne Jackson, Lou Reed, Susan Sarandon, Tim Robbins, Joan Rivers, Harvey Keitel, Chuck D, Jon Stewart, Phoebe Snow, Shirley Maclaine, Marlo Thomas, Sally Jesse Raphael, Julianne Moore, Kate Clinton and Martha Plimpton, among others.

He is currently writing and directing a musical based on the life of the fabulous international star Josephine Baker which has a score by the late Harold Arlen; **Rainbow Corner** (a musical he is collaborating on with Nathan Silver, which is about British War Brides in 1944); **Winchell**, a musical about the famous newspaper reporter, written with Keith Levenson; and the first national tour of the first musical he wrote with Richard Rodgers, **Two by Two**. Later this year (with Thomas Meehan and Peter Sipos as collaborators) audiences will see his latest musical - a revisionist's version of the Robin Hood legend. Also on the drawing board are a musical version of the cartoon, Broomhilda, and another 40's musical about Rosie the Riveter.

Charnin has received four Tony nominations, two Tony Awards, six Grammy Awards, three Emmy Awards, three Gold Records, two Platinum Records, six Drama Desk Awards, a Peabody Award for Broadcasting, and most recently another Grammy Award for Jay-Z's rap album **Hard Knock Life** which went triple platinum in 1999.

EASY STREET

Lyric by MARTIN CHARNIN
Music by CHARLES STROUSE

© 1977 EDWIN H. MORRIS & COMPANY, A Division of MPL Communications, Inc. and CHARLES STROUSE
All Rights on behalf of CHARLES STROUSE Controlled Worldwide by HELENE BLUE MUSIQUE LTD.
All Rights Reserved

ANNIE

Lyric by MARTIN CHARNIN
Music by CHARLES STROUSE

© 1977 EDWIN H. MORRIS & COMPANY, A Division of MPL Communications, Inc. and CHARLES STROUSE
All Rights on behalf of CHARLES STROUSE Controlled Worldwide by HELENE BLUE MUSIQUE LTD.
All Rights Reserved

I DON'T NEED ANYTHING BUT YOU

Lyric by MARTIN CHARNIN
Music by CHARLES STROUSE

© 1977 EDWIN H. MORRIS & COMPANY, A Division of MPL Communications, Inc. and CHARLES STROUSE
All Rights on behalf of CHARLES STROUSE Controlled Worldwide by HELENE BLUE MUSIQUE LTD.
All Rights Reserved

LITTLE GIRLS

Lyric by MARTIN CHARNIN
Music by CHARLES STROUSE

Plain Mean

Lit - tle girls, lit - tle girls, ev - 'ry-where I turn I can see them

Lit - tle girls, lit - tle girls, night and day I eat, sleep and breathe 'em. I'm an or - di - nar - y

wom - an with feel - ings. I'd like a man to nib - ble on my ear, but I ad -

© 1977 EDWIN H. MORRIS & COMPANY, A Division of MPL Communications, Inc. and CHARLES STROUSE
All Rights on behalf of CHARLES STROUSE Controlled Worldwide by HELENE BLUE MUSIQUE LTD.
All Rights Reserved

I THINK I'M GONNA LIKE IT HERE

Lyric by MARTIN CHARNIN
Music by CHARLES STROUSE

© 1977 EDWIN H. MORRIS & COMPANY, A Division of MPL Communications, Inc. and CHARLES STROUSE
All Rights on behalf of CHARLES STROUSE Controlled Worldwide by HELENE BLUE MUSIQUE LTD.
All Rights Reserved

IT'S THE HARD-KNOCK LIFE

Lyric by MARTIN CHARNIN
Music by CHARLES STROUSE

© 1977 EDWIN H. MORRIS & COMPANY, A Division of MPL Communications, Inc. and CHARLES STROUSE
All Rights on behalf of CHARLES STROUSE Controlled Worldwide by HELENE BLUE MUSIQUE LTD.
All Rights Reserved

LET'S GO TO THE MOVIES

Lyric by MARTIN CHARNIN
Music by CHARLES STROUSE

© 1981, 1982 EDWIN H. MORRIS & COMPANY, A Division of MPL Communications, Inc. and CHARLES STROUSE
All Rights on behalf of CHARLES STROUSE Controlled Worldwide by HELENE BLUE MUSIQUE LTD.
All Rights Reserved

MAYBE

Lyric by MARTIN CHARNIN
Music by CHARLES STROUSE

© 1977 EDWIN H. MORRIS & COMPANY, A Division of MPL Communications, Inc. and CHARLES STROUSE
All Rights on behalf of CHARLES STROUSE Controlled Worldwide by HELENE BLUE MUSIQUE LTD.
All Rights Reserved

A NEW DEAL FOR CHRISTMAS

Lyric by MARTIN CHARNIN
Music by CHARLES STROUSE

© 1977 EDWIN H. MORRIS & COMPANY, A Division of MPL Communications, Inc. and CHARLES STROUSE
All Rights on behalf of CHARLES STROUSE Controlled Worldwide by HELENE BLUE MUSIQUE LTD.
All Rights Reserved

47

N.Y.C.

Lyric by MARTIN CHARNIN
Music by CHARLES STROUSE

© 1977 EDWIN H. MORRIS & COMPANY, A Division of MPL Communications, Inc. and CHARLES STROUSE
All Rights on behalf of CHARLES STROUSE Controlled Worldwide by HELENE BLUE MUSIQUE LTD.
All Rights Reserved

SANDY
(Dumb Dog)

Lyric by MARTIN CHARNIN
Music by CHARLES STROUSE

© 1981, 1982 EDWIN H. MORRIS & COMPANY, A Division of MPL Communications, Inc. and CHARLES STROUSE
All Rights on behalf of CHARLES STROUSE Controlled Worldwide by HELENE BLUE MUSIQUE LTD.
All Rights Reserved

54

SIGN!

Lyric by MARTIN CHARNIN
Music by CHARLES STROUSE

© 1981, 1982 EDWIN H. MORRIS & COMPANY, A Division of MPL Communications, Inc. and CHARLES STROUSE
All Rights on behalf of CHARLES STROUSE Controlled Worldwide by HELENE BLUE MUSIQUE LTD.
All Rights Reserved

SOMETHING WAS MISSING

Lyric by MARTIN CHARNIN
Music by CHARLES STROUSE

© 1977 EDWIN H. MORRIS & COMPANY, A Division of MPL Communications, Inc. and CHARLES STROUSE
All Rights on behalf of CHARLES STROUSE Controlled Worldwide by HELENE BLUE MUSIQUE LTD.
All Rights Reserved

TOMORROW

Lyric by MARTIN CHARNIN
Music by CHARLES STROUSE

© 1977 EDWIN H. MORRIS & COMPANY, A Division of MPL Communications, Inc. and CHARLES STROUSE
All Rights on behalf of CHARLES STROUSE Controlled Worldwide by HELENE BLUE MUSIQUE LTD.
All Rights Reserved

WE GOT ANNIE

Lyric by MARTIN CHARNIN
Music by CHARLES STROUSE

© 1977, 1981, 1982 EDWIN H. MORRIS & COMPANY, A Division of MPL Communications, Inc. and CHARLES STROUSE
All Rights on behalf of CHARLES STROUSE Controlled Worldwide by HELENE BLUE MUSIQUE LTD.
All Rights Reserved

Spoken: We Got An-nie!

WE'D LIKE TO THANK YOU HERBERT HOOVER

Lyric by MARTIN CHARNIN
Music by CHARLES STROUSE

© 1977 EDWIN H. MORRIS & COMPANY, A Division of MPL Communications, Inc. and CHARLES STROUSE
All Rights on behalf of CHARLES STROUSE Controlled Worldwide by HELENE BLUE MUSIQUE LTD.
All Rights Reserved

YOU WON'T BE AN ORPHAN FOR LONG

Lyric by MARTIN CHARNIN
Music by CHARLES STROUSE

© 1977 EDWIN H. MORRIS & COMPANY, A Division of MPL Communications, Inc. and CHARLES STROUSE
All Rights on behalf of CHARLES STROUSE Controlled Worldwide by HELENE BLUE MUSIQUE LTD.
All Rights Reserved

77

YOU'RE NEVER FULLY DRESSED WITHOUT A SMILE

Lyric by MARTIN CHARNIN
Music by CHARLES STROUSE

Tempo Di Ted Lewis

Hey, ho - bo man, Hey, Dap - per Dan, You both_ got your style, But broth - er, You're nev - er ful - ly dressed with - out a smile!_____ Your clothes_ may be

© 1977 EDWIN H. MORRIS & COMPANY, A Division of MPL Communications, Inc. and CHARLES STROUSE
All Rights on behalf of CHARLES STROUSE Controlled Worldwide by HELENE BLUE MUSIQUE LTD.
All Rights Reserved